THE ESSENTIAL
VITAM...

GW00362093

PHILLIP DAY & NICHOLAS COCKAYNE

 Credence Publications

The Essential Guide to Vitamin C

Copyright © 2010
Phillip Day and Nicholas Cockayne

The right of Phillip Day and Nicholas Cockayne to be
identified as the Authors of the Work has been asserted by
them in accordance with the Copyright, Designs and Patents
Act 1988.

Print history
First print 2010

Caution: Please note that the information contained in this
booklet is for educational purposes only and should not be
construed as medical advice. A properly qualified physician
should always be consulted in the matter of serious illness.

ISBN 1-904015-26-3

Manufactured in Great Britain
Credence Publications
PO Box 3
TONBRIDGE
Kent TN12 9ZY UK
www.credence.org

1st ed

TABLE OF CONTENTS

"I know that most men, including those at ease with problems of the greatest complexity, can seldom accept even the simplest and most obvious truth if it would oblige them to admit the falsity of conclusions which they have delighted in explaining to colleagues, proudly taught to others, and which they have woven, thread by thread, into the fabric of their lives."
– Leo Tolstoy

"I have never seen a patient that vitamin C would not benefit."
– FR Klenner MD, pioneer in vitamin C research

"Science is the search for truth - it is not a game in which one tries to beat his opponent, to do harm to others."
– Linus Pauling PhD, two-time Nobel laureate, pioneer of vitamin C treatments

"Nor does wealth and rich food necessarily protect against lack of vitamins. I remember my contact with one of the wealthiest royal families of Europe where the young prince had a constant temperature and had poor health. Upon administering vitamin C, the condition readily cleared up."
– Albert Szent-Gyorgyi MD, PhD, Nobel laureate, discoverer/isolator of vitamin C

"Disease is cured by the body itself, not by doctors or remedies."
- John Harvey Kellogg, MD

"The doctor of the future will give no medicine, but will interest his or her patients in the care of the human frame, in a proper diet, and in the cause and prevention of disease."
- Thomas A Edison

INTRODUCTION

Despite constant advances in science and surgical medicine, our society is suffering more disease and illness than ever before. Yet research into these conditions, some of which are the most prolific killers of our age, has been, and continues to be stymied at every turn. Perhaps harsh words, but true?

This booklet aims to provide you with an overview of the research which has uncovered the benefits and uses of vitamin C, a vitamin that is absolutely essential for keeping you healthy, preventing illness and fighting disease, but which has no serious commercial advantage. We hope you find the information enlightening and a valuable aid in your fight for a healthy future. While the medical establishment repeatedly fails with surgical and drug-based treatments for disease, peer-reviewed evidence going back decades reveals a different story. That orthomolecular medicine, which is therapeutic nutrition, offers the most effective approach to ills, and when combined with diet and lifestyle changes with the patient's full co-operation, presents extraordinary breakthroughs in conditions previously thought incurable.

THE FAILURE OF MEDICINE

"It's supposed to be a secret but I'll tell you anyway. We doctors do nothing. We only help and encourage the doctor within."
– Albert Schweitzer MD

The mainstream media constantly reminds us that modern medicine is the pinnacle of scientific achievement. And while it is true that scientists have made some great advances, progress in other areas has been a downright disgrace. On the plus side, doctors are able to perform heart transplants, face transplants, keyhole surgery and prescribe drugs for almost every medical condition. Science has made excellent strides in A&E trauma medicine, infant survivability at birth, prosthesis and pain management, so the impression is that doctors are punching far above their weight and keeping us in better health these days than at any previous point in history.

It's a surprise, therefore, to learn that modern medicine has dropped the ball in one of the most vital realms of medical care – disease – and that the medical fraternity has become the third leading cause of death in the western world in most industrial nations, with the exception of the United States of America, where doctors are now the leading cause of death. How can this be?[1] Even physicians themselves are perishing in ever increasing numbers from the very diseases they are trying to cure in others, in which there has been little to no progress made in prevention. In the Credence title *Health Wars*, we show how western healthcare has become a killer for the very reason that it declines to adopt the metabolic model and concentrate on nutrition and lifestyle as the primary strategy for preventing and combating disease. If you also include the deliberate refusal by our medical czars to spread life-saving information to prevent killers number 1 & 2 (heart disease and cancer), you now have a 'healthcare' system consuming

---

[1] **Day, Phillip** *Health Wars,* Credence, 2007

prodigious amounts of taxpayer money as the leading cause of death of those taxpayers today.[2]

Yes, it's about money. Sickness is big business and no-one's making much money in health. In fact, crises in general are a socialist's perfect excuse for raising taxes, ratcheting more power away from the citizen, and punishing us when we don't conform. We see this pattern played out daily in our newspapers over genuine or manufactured crises in war, the economy, social affairs like poverty and crime, 'global warming' and medicine. American critic and writer H L Mencken put it this way:

> "The whole aim of practical politics is to keep the population alarmed and hence clamorous to be led to safety, by menacing it with an endless series of hobgoblins, all of them imaginary."

The more 'crises' in health, the more money can justifiably be stolen by government and industry to 'protect' the citizen. We've seen this with such emblems of medical stupidity as HIV, SARS, foot and mouth, swine flu, bird flu, SMON, measles, mumps and rubella. Tomorrow, who knows? What the public is not being told in a way that would make them sit up and take note is that vitamins, minerals, essential fats, diet, lack of stress and exercise *will* take care of most medical problems and even stop them occurring in the first place. You're not being told this because it's economically unviable. The economies of certain leading industrial nations today rely as much on disease for economic stability as war.

Politicians lying to us, imagine that. Actually, *not* telling someone the truth is not the same thing as lying to them. You can get into trouble for telling a lie but rarely get sent to the headmaster's study for *omitting* to say something. In the meantime, the more disasters you can drum up with poverty, energy, war and 'healthcare', the bigger the budgets that can be crafted to deal with them. The trouble is, the methods medicine comes up with for 'healing us' often do fierce violence to those most vulnerable in our society. *Associated Press* reported in 2006:

---

[2] Ibid.

Harmful reactions to some of the most widely used medicines — from insulin to a common antibiotic — sent more than 700,000 Americans to emergency rooms each year, landmark government research shows.[3]

The UK's *Daily Mail,* 11th January 2010, writes:

THE 'FALSE' PANDEMIC: DRUG FIRMS CASHED IN ON SCARE OVER SWINE FLU, CLAIMS EURO HEALTH CHIEF

The swine flu outbreak was a 'false pandemic' driven by drug companies that stood to make billions of pounds from a worldwide scare, a leading health expert has claimed. Wolfgang Wodarg, head of health at the Council of Europe, accused the makers of flu drugs and vaccines of influencing the World Health Organisation's decision to declare a pandemic.

Environment and Health News made sobering reading in 1998:

Australians may want to think twice before their next trip to the clinic. The chances of dying in hospital, or suffering some injury while there, stand at around 16% in Australia. Half this risk is due to doctor or hospital error – which means that 8% of hospital patients are accidentally killed or injured by the staff.[4]

In an emailed response to the *British Medical Journal* (BMJ), Ron Law, Executive Director of the National Nutritional Foods Association (NNFA) in New Zealand and a member of the New Zealand Ministry of Health Working Group advising on medical error, cites the following statistics and facts: Official Australian government reports reveal that preventable medical error in hospitals is responsible for 11% of all deaths in Australia, which is about 1 of every 9 deaths.[5] [6] If deaths from properly researched, properly registered, properly prescribed and properly used drugs

---

[3] Associated Press, 17th October 2006. www.msnbc.msn.com/id/15305033/

[4] *Environment and Health News,* vol.3, January 1998

[5] **www.mercola.com** *Iatrogenic Injury in Australia* - This is the executive summary of a 150-page official report revealing 14,000 preventable medical error deaths (only in hospitals - not private practice). (Full report at www.mercola.com).

[6] Australian Bureau of Statistics - Australian 1994 total deaths (1994) = 126,692, www.mercola.com, op. cit.

were added along with preventable deaths due to private practice, it comes to a staggering 19%, which is almost 1 of every 5 deaths.

The New Zealand figures are very similar, says Law. He states that over the past decade the equivalent of New Zealand's second largest city (Christchurch) has been killed by preventable medical error, and its biggest city, Auckland, as an example, either killed or maimed from properly researched and registered drugs across Australasia.

Dr Joseph Mercola, who hosts one of the most comprehensive health sites on the Internet, has analysed Law's statistics:

"More than 5 million people have been killed by Western medical practice in the past decade (Europe, USA, Canada, Australia, and NZ) and 20 million killed or permanently maimed. Put another way, the economic impact of deaths due to preventable medical error and deaths from properly researched, properly registered, properly prescribed and properly used drugs is approximately $1 trillion over the past decade. Law notes that only 0.3% of these deaths are properly coded and classified in official statistics as being attributed to these causes." [7]

Unacceptable

Death from mass quackery was abruptly brought to the public's attention when consumer advocate Ralph Nader reported in the early 1990's that around 300,000 Americans were being killed by doctors and hospitals *each year*. This is almost six times the number of active servicemen who perished in the entire Vietnam War *dying each year* at the hands of their doctors. Remember the mass demonstrations and huge outpourings of anger over the war? Where was this indignance against medicine? Was Nader wrong?

Unfortunately not. The *Journal of the American Medical Association* figures largely agree and are tabulated as follows:

---

[7] *British Medical Journal,* November 11, 2000; 321: 1178A (emailed response)

UNITED STATES IATROGENIC DEATHS PER YEAR

Unnecessary surgery	12,000[8]
Medication errors in hospital	7,000[9]
Miscellaneous errors in hospitals	20,000[10]
Infections in hospitals	80,000[11]
Non-error, negative effects of drugs	106,000[12]
Total:	**225,000**

The above does not include the number of cancer, heart disease, stroke and diabetes cases that could have been avoided if medicine promoted prevention instead of cure. The JAMA data[13] were compiled by Dr Barbara Starfield[14] of Baltimore's Johns Hopkins School of Hygiene and Public Health, who describes how the US healthcare system is contributing to a shameful, iatrogenic catastrophe of monstrous proportions. Starfield offers several warnings in interpreting these numbers. Firstly, most of the data are derived from studies of hospitalised patients only. Secondly, these estimates are for deaths only and do not include negative effects associated with disability or discomfort. That the long-term fatal effects of some of these botched procedures are not included implies, of course, that the real tally is far higher.

Great care is taken to keep these figures from the public for obvious reasons, and the whitewash has been largely successful. How many people are happy to give money to cancer or diabetes

---

[8] **Leape, L** "Unnecessary surgery", *Annu Rev. Public Health*, 1992; 13:363-383

[9] **Phillips D, Christenfeld N & L Glynn** "Increase in US medication-error deaths between 1983 and 1993", *Lancet*, 1998;351:643-644

[10] **Lazarou J, Pomeranz B & P Corey** "Incidence of adverse drug reactions in hospitalized patients", *JAMA*, 1998;279:1200-1205

[11] Lazarou J, Pomeranz B, Corey P., op. cit.

[12] **Kohn L, ed, Corrigan J, ed, Donaldson M, ed.** "To Err Is Human: Building a Safer Health System", Washington, DC: National Academy Press; 1999

[13] *Journal American Medical Association*, vol.284, 26th July 2000

[14] **B Starfield** Department of Health Policy and Management, Johns Hopkins School of Hygiene and Public Health, 624 N Broadway, Room 452, Baltimore, MD 21205-1996

charities, leave part of their estate to these organisations and even leap out of a perfectly serviceable aircraft at 14,000 feet with a hanky strapped to their back to 'raise money for leukaemia? They never ask where the research money goes or to what purpose it is being put. They naively assume the genuine progress made in other areas is being replicated to cure the cancer which killed their Dad. Sadly, human nature being what it is, there are more people today making a living out of cancer than are dying from it, so cancer research has little interest in killing the goose that lays the golden egg.[15] We know this from their dismissal of any approach unsanctioned by the pharmaceutical industry. Put another way, why, from an economic view alone, would anyone ever wish to cure cancer? There are billions invested in specialist oncology units around the world, cancer hospitals, radiology equipment and staff, cancer drugs, charities and their clothes shops. Chemotherapy alone is an $11 billion business. Millions would have to retrain.

Why are more people dying of cancer today than ever before if there's so much progress being made? The same goes for heart disease, stroke, diabetes and a dozen other conditions. The newspapers trumpet the weekly 'life-saving' drug or the good news that the cancer war is being won. In reality, the five-year or better survival rates for almost all forms of cancer remain largely unchanged for the past forty years. *Why?* After all the billions spent and 'cancer wars' declared, is it that we haven't found the answers to these killers yet, or that the answers just don't pay?

Can't see the wood for the trees

The good news is, the answers are known and they revolve around nutrition, stress, exercise and toxicity. So far as nutrition is concerned, everyone agrees that you are what you eat, yet doctors are required to swallow the incredible paradox that food is good enough to keep you alive and make every cell in your body but not good enough to fix you when you're sick. Nutrition is routinely ignored because raw vegetables and vitamin C don't make Porsche

---

[15] **Griffin, G E** *World Without Cancer,* American Media, 1996

payments, nor pay the huge dividends speculators expect from investing in drug stocks. Walk into a hospital at lunchtime and it's quite clear nobody has the slightest clue what food will do to the human body. Why would a pharmaceutical company investigate commercially worthless vitamins, when to do so would threaten their drug revenues? It is no coincidence that doctors receive almost no formal training in nutrition since they are trained in institutions funded by the drug industry. Welcome to the revolving door. Next time you visit your GP, ask him how much nutritional training he got at med school. His answer might surprise you if he doesn't hound you out of his surgery first.

Two different belief systems

Complementary and orthodox medicine are two opposing philosophies. In orthodox/drug medicine, nature is weak. The body and mind are treated separately. The body usually cannot heal itself without intervention by the doctor and his life-saving medicines. Symptoms are treated, not the underlying cause. The physician is the unquestioned authority. There are a myriad of different medical specialties, depending on the affected organ of the body.

By contrast, in complementary medicine nature is strong and the body has a tremendous ability for self-healing – The Doctor Within. Body and mind are intricately connected and the approach to healing integrates the two. Here, the physician is really a bystander, assisting and advising the patient on how to help themselves recover. Patients have an important part to play in this process by taking control over their treatment decisions. They take responsibility for their illness. They research their afflictions thoroughly. They work in conjunction with properly trained health practitioners to apply natural and effective strategies their body can use to heal itself. They apply these strategies consistently, maintain a positive attitude and never give up. Of course, drugs can be used where required, but never as a matter of primary resort with disease.

Nutritional treatments are popular with the public because the approach makes sense, the materials used have few side-effects, and

11

people quickly feel better. The careers of Drs. Klenner, Cathcart, McCormick and Riordan have demonstrated since the 1940's that vitamin C, for instance, when used in correct therapeutic dosages, can combat the deadliest of diseases with few side-effects. Vitamin B3 has been used to great effect with depression and schizophrenia, vitamin B6 and zinc for emotional problems, vitamin D for just about everything, vitamin E and magnesium for epilepsy, and vitamin F, the polyunsaturated fatty acids, for ADHD, cancer and a host of other problems.

So, food can fix you – official. Or rather, Albert Schweitzer's 'The Doctor Within' fixes you. You'd think our medical peers would be cock-a-hoop at such news. You'd think they'd be dancing over Westminster Bridge from St Thomas's, punching the air with their stethoscopes and uncorking the Bollinger. You'd be wrong. Only stiff silence greets the power in the molecules. Lips compress into thin lines. Eyes droop to contemplate shoes. Doctors overtly betraying the pharma-gods are dragged before medical councils with all the ardour of Loyola's Inquisition. The Doctor Within is an importunate profit-wrecker. Heretics are fined, de-licensed or go to jail. Most patients have no idea any of this goes on, though the first clue they get is when they mention 'nutrition' to their oncologist in all innocence and watch those knuckles whiten.

Welcome to the truth hour. Andrew Saul PhD, who has spent most of his professional career in the vanguard of this research, gives a suitable, exasperated introduction for vitamin C:

"What is it about a little left-handed molecule of six carbons, six oxygens, and eight hydrogens that ticks off so many in the medical community?"[16]

Let's find out.

---

[16] www.orthomolecular.org

WHAT IS VITAMIN C?

"Intensive research ... has convinced me that the human organism can protect itself against infection virtually completely by proper nutrition."
- Dr B P Sandler

Vitamin C is an essential nutrient for the human body. Wikipedia describes it chemically as 2-oxo-L-threo-hexono-1,4-lactone-2,3-enediol, or L-ascorbic acid, L-ascorbate or $C_6H_8O_6$ – take your pick. It has a molecular mass of 176.14 grams and is so named for its active properties in fighting scurvy (*a* meaning 'no' and *scorbutus* 'scurvy').

Vitamin C is a form of sugar acid that appears white to yellow in a crystal or powder form and is water-soluble. It is found most famously in citrus fruits but also in leafy greens, a staple ingredient used to fortify foods, and is familiar to many as a childhood vitamin supplement, one of the most important for your continued wellbeing.

It is unfortunate then, that while it is synthesised internally by all but a few mammals, humans suffer from a genetic deficiency which prevents us from generating vitamin C in our bodies. Whereas most mammals can synthesise this vital nutrient with glucose produced from glycogen by enzymes in the liver,[17] our only hope of getting C is through our diet. An associate of Pauling's, Dr Matthias Rath, comments:

"Animals don't get heart attacks because they produce vitamin C in their bodies, which protects their blood vessel walls. In humans, unable to produce vitamin C (a condition known as hypoascorbemia), dietary vitamin deficiency weakens these walls. Cardiovascular disease is an early form of scurvy. Clinical studies document that optimum daily intakes of vitamins and other essential nutrients halt and reverse coronary heart disease naturally.

---

[17] **Bánhegyi G, Mándl J** "The hepatic glycogenoreticular system", *Pathol Oncol Res* 7 (2): 2001, pp.107–110

The single most important difference between the metabolism of human beings and most other living species is the dramatic difference in the body pool of vitamin C. The body reservoir of vitamin C in people is on average 10 to 100 times lower than the vitamin C levels in animals."[18]

Lucky for us the human body is an astounding system with a remarkable capacity for self-regulation and correction. DNA itself is a three-out-of-four, error-correcting digital code with stop and start bits to parse the assembly instructions of every protein of an organism. Unlike the 4,000 or so species of mammal which produce vitamin C internally, the human genetic code compensates for our defect by having red blood cells specifically designed for increased absorption of C. Haemoglobin is able to absorb the oxidised version of the nutrient, deoxidise it in the cell, then transport the active 'antioxidant' to where it is most needed.[19] Red blood cells ensure our bodies are kept adequately supplied, and are even able to recycle the nutrient to some degree. There's just one hitch. We've got to eat or drink vitamin C to get it into the system in the first place. What a disappointment, then, that our peers don't do more to ensure everyone is fully briefed.

When was the last time someone told you on TV that cooking destroys vitamin C? Never. How many times on TV has a 'celebrity' chef shown you more inventive ways to murder your food with heat? Five times a night, and they swear at you for getting it wrong. So what percentage of see-no-evil, hear-no-evil humanity goes through an entire British, American and Australian winter cooking everything and ending up sicker than Gordon Ramsey's dog? The vast majority. How many are destined to end up dying of a disease not even their livestock are dying from? The vast majority. How many will be talked into taking 'life-saving' drugs and other redundant nostrums before they finally expire? The vast majority.

Room for a little improvement, wouldn't you say?

---

[18] **Rath, M** *Why Animals Don't Get Heart Attacks – But People Do!* MR Publishing, 2000, p.10
[19] *How Humans Make Up For An 'Inborn' Vitamin C Deficiency.* www.sciencedaily.com/releases/2008/03/080320120726.htm

Not just an acid
Dr Tim O'Shea writes:

"Most sources equate vitamin C with ascorbic acid, as though they were the same thing. They're not. Ascorbic acid is an isolate, a fraction, a distillate of naturally occurring vitamin C. In addition to ascorbic acid, vitamin C must include rutin, bioflavonoids, Factor K, Factor J, Factor P, Tyrosinase, Ascorbinogen, In addition, mineral co-factors must be available in proper amounts. If any of these parts are missing, there is no vitamin C, no vitamin activity. When some of them are present, the body will draw on its own stores to make up the differences, so that the whole vitamin may be present. Only then will vitamin activity take place, provided that all other conditions and co-factors are present. Ascorbic acid is described merely as the "antioxidant wrapper" portion of vitamin C; ascorbic acid protects the functional parts of the vitamin from rapid oxidation or breakdown."[20]

So vitamin C is a complex. The ascorbic acid and ascorbate (an ion of ascorbic acid) are required for a variety of essential metabolic functions. They help metabolise fats and proteins and aid recovery from wounds. In addition to vitamin E and two amino acids, lysine and proline, vitamin C is vital for the creation of collagen, the chief protein in soft and connective tissue throughout the body. Vitamin C, therefore, helps provide us with skin, hair, corneas, tendons, muscles, ligaments, bones, organs, cartilage, and the basis for the very structure of our cells. Without it we simply fall apart, which is scurvy. Last but not least, vitamin C strengthens the piping of our cardiovascular system, and its deficiency is one of the chief factors in the leading cause of disease death today, heart disease, which destroys one in every two and half of us (if you can picture such a creature). And in 50% of those deaths, Andrew Saul reminds us, the first symptom *is* death.[21] An adequate level of vitamin C in the diet, therefore, is vital over the long-term. Failure to do this gets you dead. Badly.

---

[20] www.thedoctorwithin.com
[21] www.orthomolecular.org

What is it good for?

Like a good Toyota, you get your mileage with vitamin C. It's a powerful antihistamine, antiviral, antitoxin, and Halle Berry uses the powdered stuff mixed with water to exfoliate her First Division visage. And, as if all that's not good enough, vitamin C acts as a particularly effective antioxidant, neutralising cell-damaging free radicals or oxidative elements in the body.

As we age, we slowly oxidise (biologically 'rust'). An antioxidant is a type of molecule able to slow down or prevent this oxidation process. Oxidation itself is a chemical reaction crucial to life, but one that can be damaging too. The body employs various reducing agents and enzymes in order to control this vital but potentially harmful system. If not properly controlled, oxidation releases adverse levels of peroxides and free radicals which damage the cell and its DNA. Antioxidants like vitamin C stop these reactions by removing the free radicals and becoming oxidised themselves. If there are more free radicals than the antioxidants and enzymes can control, the body suffers oxidative stress, which can induce diabetes, cardiovascular disease, hypertension, and chronic inflammatory diseases. Vitamin C is a major player in preventing this from occurring.

Linus Pauling PhD, often known as the 'Father of Vitamin C' and twice awarded the Nobel Prize, declared that large intakes of up to 10 g of vitamin C each day aids anti-cancer activity within the body. It also assists in repairing damaged arteries and removing arterial plaque for heart disease sufferers. Pauling was largely derided for making these statements, and we'll examine the controversies in a minute, yet he lived into his nineties. Today, much higher doses of C complex are used by many practitioners for cancer/heart/stroke patients in nutritional therapy who believe Pauling was right, and that the popular nutrient is indispensable to the body in its fight to regain health.

Dietary sources of vitamin C - fruit and veg

Vitamin C is found in abundance in fruits and vegetables, and also in some meats. Rose hips, blackcurrant, peppers, kiwi, guava, broccoli, and nature's most maligned Christmas treat, the Brussels sprout, are all high in vitamin C. Not only are these foods packed with nutrients in their organic form (unlike meat), they are low in fat and do not need to be cooked to be eaten. If you wish to destroy all the nutrients, enzymes and vitamin C that make fruit and vegetables healthy in the first place, simply fire up the pan and cook 'em.

Bioflavonoids

Dr Albert Szent-Gyorgi, 1937 Nobel laureate for his isolation of vitamin C, later found other factors intrinsic to the action of C. Originally believed to be a single nutrient, Vitamin C became the subject of further testing by Szent-Gyorgi, who fought long and hard to have the co-factor (bio)flavonoids included.

Bioflavonoids are derived from plant pigments known as flavonols and flavones and are found in many of the same fruits and vegetables rich in vitamin C. Szent-Gyorgi argued that they were essential to human health and coined the new bioflavonoids 'Vitamin P'. Though they are widely accepted today for their health benefits and are available in hydroxylated and methoxylated forms, the term 'Vitamin P' was less well received by our medical czars.

Bioflavonoids have great antioxidant properties but in a different way to C. While the body welcomes ascorbic acid and the ascorbates, it recognises bioflavonoids as a foreign compound and acts quickly to flush them from the system. This increases levels of uric acid and serves to expel excess free radicals and other toxins from the body, aiding in the antioxidant process. While different kinds of bioflavonoid help the body in different ways, all are extremely useful. Those found in citrus fruits increase the absorption of vitamin C in our cells, aid blood vessel permeability and blood flow, and exhibit anti-allergy, anti-inflammatory, anti-microbial and anti-cancer properties. In a nutshell? Bioflavonoids are seriously good for you.

Meat

Certain meats also contain vitamin C. This is because some animals have high internal levels of C which build up in certain

17

tissues. Liver is the best source of meat for C, but loses up to 100% of its C content when cooked. Unfortunately, the muscles that make up the bulk of western carnivorous diets also happen to be the cuts of meat with the lowest concentrations of vitamin C. We don't like to eat meat raw. Carnivores do.

In 1928, the Arctic anthropologist Vilhjalmur Stefansson emulated the Inuit diet to test a theory. Despite having almost no plant material in their diet, the native people avoided scurvy while European explorers suffered heavily. Both ate meat-based diets. Living exclusively on only lightly cooked meat for a year without any ill-effects, Stefansson was able to prove that cooking the meat destroyed specific nutrients within, later discovered to be vitamin C.

Milk

Milk also contains useful amounts of C for breast-feeding babies. Mums who have good levels in their own bodies produce milk twice as fortified with the nutrient than found in raw cow's or goat's milk. Once pasteurised, milk loses most of its C content. Although baby formulas boast that they are fortified with vitamins and just as good as breast milk, the heating and storage that goes with such products wrecks the vitamin C content. Formula well fortified with vitamin C might well contain very little after transit, storage and heating. Nature knows best.

Supplements

Diets being what they are these days, not everyone chooses to get their vitamin C through eating raw fruit and veg, nor chomping lightly cooked slivers of liver. Many choose the world's most popular vitamin supplement instead – you guessed it, vitamin C. Available in caplets, powders, capsules, multivitamin and antioxidant formulations, C supplements are many and varied. If you choose to take a vitamin C supplement, ensure your intake is spread throughout the day to maximise absorption and that the supplement contains bioflavonoids to aid vitamin C metabolism. Steven Hickey PhD writes:

"An individual who wanted protection from, say, the common cold by taking vitamin C, would raise their blood levels more effectively by taking divided doses or slow-release formulations.... If a single dose of vitamin C raises blood levels for about six hours or one quarter of the day, the subject is unprotected for the other three quarters of the time.... The biochemical data supports Pauling's hypothesis that, for a large proportion of the population, the optimal dose of vitamin C is several grams a day.... A single megadose tablet will only raise blood levels for a short period and is likely to be therapeutically ineffective. The aim is to raise plasma levels consistently and this requires either multiple tablets taken at short intervals throughout the day, or the use of slow-release formulations." [22]

Conclusion

Although the levels of vitamin C in food depend on the type of plant, the soil it grew in, freshness, how it was stored or prepared, etc., the following guidelines will ensure a good dietary intake of vitamin C can be achieved.

Raw food rocks! Cooking and heating destroys many of the active components of vitamin C. If you boil a saucepan of vegetables for too long you risk having more vitamin C in the pan water than the food. Copper cooking vessels also reduce the C content of your food.

Fresh is best! As food is stored, the vitamin C content gradually decomposes. An orange in your lounge fruit bowl will lose 50% of its vitamin C content in two weeks. The fresher the food, the more vitamin C it will retain. Correct storage in a cool place, such as a refrigerator, also helps maintain vitamin C content.

Fruit and veg! A diet comprising 80% plant-based, organic fruits and vegetables with 60%-plus consumed raw is the way to go. Vegetable juices are highly recommended – more so than fruit juices, which contain concentrated sugar and acid. Patients recovering from serious illness would do well to keep their raw food ratio high, and vegetable juices enable them to achieve this quickly and effortlessly.

---

[22] **Hickey S and H Roberts** *Ascorbate,* Lulu, 2004

HOW MUCH IS ENOUGH?

"Learn and live. If you don't, you won't."
– US Army training film, WW II

Given that vitamin C is so essential to human health, why does it stir up such acrimony in the science community? While vitamin C is accepted as a vital part of a healthy diet, mainstream healthcare refuses to acknowledge the nutrient's mega-dose therapeutic role. It's an intellectually inconsistent argument chiefly brought on by the widespread ignorance of nutritional medicine. The experts all agree on one thing about vitamin C, however. That the recommended daily allowance (RDA) should be set at a level so low that nobody will be in any possible danger of deriving any benefit from it:

UK Food Standards Agency - 75 mg per day
World Health Organisation[23] - 45 mg per day
Health Canada[24] - 60 mg per day
US National Academy of Sciences - 60-95 mg per day

Worse, medical and government agencies claim the average person gets all the vitamin C they need 'from a generally balanced diet', yet the majority of diets in the industrialised world are hardly 'balanced' (whatever the word means in this context), and if you cook your food you're done, so far as vitamin C is concerned. Processed meats, additive-heavy, sugar-rich factory foods, dairy products, and high-carbohydrate fatty foods make up the bulk of what we're wolfing down before the mad dash into work. And did we mention that if you are stressed, your body sacrifices vitamin C as the catalyst for the production of adrenalin, which means that you may well be taking in the recommended daily allowance of C, but then stripping it out if you're stressed or ill. Moreover, if you are pregnant, injured, diseased or otherwise health-compromised, your

---

[23] http://whqlibdoc.who.int/publications/2004/9241546123_chap7.pdf
[24] www.hc-sc.gc.ca/dhp-mps/prodnatur/applications/licen-prod/monograph/mono_vitamin_ c-eng.php

body's requirement for vitamin C rockets, according to Hilary Roberts PhD, co-author of *Ascorbate:*

"Stressed and even mildly ill people can tolerate 1,000 times more vitamin C, implying a change in biochemistry that was ignored in creating the RDA. In setting the RDA, unsubstantiated risks of taking too much vitamin C have been accorded great importance, whereas the risks of not taking enough have been ignored. Real scientists understand that 'no scientific proof' is a fancy way of saying 'we don't like this idea.'"[25]

Proof of the pudding

Dr G C Willis demonstrated that vitamin C complex could reverse atherosclerosis. Willis gave a sample of his patients 1.5 g a day and gave the remainder no vitamin C at all. After a year, the atherosclerotic deposits in the patients fed the vitamin C had decreased in 30% of the cases. In contrast, no reduction in deposits was observed in the control group, which had grown further. Sadly, in spite of clear evidence over 40 years ago of the benefits of even these small doses of C, no follow-up study was ever commissioned.[26]

Professor Gey, from the University of Basel in Switzerland, conducted studies in which he compared the vitamin C, vitamin A (beta carotene) and cholesterol intakes of citizens living in northern Europe with their counterparts in the southern regions of the continent. He found:

➢ Those living in the northern nations had the highest levels of cardiovascular disease and lowest blood levels of vitamins

➢ Southern European populations had the reverse statistics of their northern counterparts and were much more healthy

➢ Optimum intakes of vitamins C, E and A had far greater impact on decreasing risks of cardiovascular disease than the reduction of cholesterol, now becoming increasingly viewed (correctly) as a secondary factor in heart-disease risk (an inevitable result of

---

[25] www.doctoryourself.com
[26] **Willis G C, Light A W & W S Gow** "Serial arteriography in atherosclerosis", *Canadian Medical Association Journal* (1954) 71: pp.562-568

the primary deficiency of nutrients leading to the breakdown of arterial walls)

Gey's report also highlighted the preference for the Mediterranean diet, rich in wine and olive oil, abundant in bioflavonoids and vitamin E, as a main prevention regimen for heart disease in almost all its forms.[27]

Further studies showed that these nutrients *separately* produced impressive results for cardiac disease prevention:

➢ Vitamin C intake lowers cardiovascular risk by 50%[28] [29]

➢ Vitamin E intake lowers cardiovascular risk by one-third, documented in 87,000 study participants over six years[30]

➢ Beta carotene (vitamin A) intake lowers cardiovascular risk over 30%, documented in more than 87,000 study participants over six years

➢ No prescription drug has ever come close to matching these figures in preventing heart disease[31]

However, when these nutrients were combined with other synergistic agents, such as magnesium, vitamin B3 (nicotinic acid), vitamin B5 (pantothenate) and the amino acid carnitine, and levels of these maintained in the body over the long-term, near total prevention could be expected, and in those already suffering from a

---

[27] **Gey K F, Puska P, Jordan P & U K Moser** "Inverse correlation between plasma Vitamin E and mortality from ischemic heart disease in cross-cultural epidemiology", *American Journal of Clinical Nutrition* (1991) 53: p.326, supplement

[28] **Ginter E** "Vitamin C deficiency cholesterol metabolism and atherosclerosis", *Journal of Orthomolecular Medicine* (1991) 6:166-173; **Ginter E**, "Marginal vitamin C deficiency, lipid metabolism and atherosclerosis", *Lipid Research* (1978) 16: pp.216-220

[29] **Harwood H J Jr, Greene Y J & P W Stacpoole** "Inhibition of human leucocyte 3-hydroxy-3-methylglutaryl coenzyme A reductase activity by ascorbic acid. An effect mediated by the free radical monodehydro-ascorbate", *Journal of Biological Chemistry* (1986) 261: pp.7127-7135

[30] **Beamish R** "Vitamin E – then and now", *Canadian Journal of Cardiology* (1993) 9: pp. 29-31

[31] Rath, Matthias, *Why Animals...* op. cit. p.53

variety of cardiac ailments, a clear record of efficacy in reversing these conditions was consistently observed. [32] [33] [34] [35]

Scurvy in the industrial nations is rare (vitamin C depletion), even with the ghastly diets we feed ourselves today. However, long-term C *deficiency* is common in many, hence the prevalence of heart disease, cancer and stroke in their various forms.

Heading in the right direction

We started off believing in the 60 mg RDA, gulping down Nurse's Haliborange tablet at school, and wondering why we still got measles and flu. Then along come a bunch of doctors saying, 'Why not try more vitamin C – up around 1,000 – 3,000 mg a day?" The public cringed, believing that anything therapeutically valuable had to be lethal in higher doses because drugs were, and yet a surprising thing happened. When people began taking more vitamin C, they got better *faster*.

So scientists cottoned onto the metabolic deficiency concept, that nutrients only acted as curatives for diseases if they were *maintained* in the body. If you use vitamin C to cure a scurvy patient from collagen collapse, and then withdraw the curative because no-one takes a cure for life, the person gets scurvy again! The conclusion, obviously, is that vitamins can cure disease by rectifying the nutritional deficiency, and the more of a vitamin you give someone who's deficient in it, the faster the recovery from the condition. But

[32] **Sokolov B, Hori M, Saelhof C C, Wrzolek T & T Imai** "Aging, atherosclerosis and ascorbic acid metabolism", *Journal of the American Gerontology Society* (1966) 14: 1239-1260

[33] **Opie L H** "Role of carnitine in fatty acid metabolism of normal and ischemic myocardium", *American Heart Journal* (1979) 97: pp.375-388

[34] **Avogaro P, Bon G B & M Fusello** "Effect of pantethine on lipids, lipoproteins and apolipoproteins in man", *Current Therapeutic Research* (1983) 33: pp.488-493

[35] **Altschul R, Hoffer A & J D Stephen** "Influence of nicotinic acid on serum cholesterol in man", *Archives of Biochemistry and Biophysics* (1955) 54: pp.558-559; **Carlson L A, Hamsten A & A Asplund** "Pronounced lowering of serum levels of lipoprotein Lp(a) in hyperlipidemic subjects treated with nicotinic acid", *Journal of Internal Medicine (England)* (1989) 226: 271-276

the nutrient must be maintained in the diet for life, as one would expect. This has been noted with beriberi (thiamine B1 deficiency), pellagra, schizophrenia and depression (niacin B3 deficiency), pernicious anaemia (cyanocobalamin B12 deficiency), and so on.

The next question is, given the fact that our bodies require a much greater concentration of vitamin C if we're ailing from trauma, injury or cell damage,[36] how much *should* we be taking? Drs. Hickey and Roberts list out the following guideline on dosage. Notice that the government-recommended daily allowance (RDA) is considered a sub-clinical deficiency!

Dosage effects

Acute deficiency means ascorbate intake is extremely low, leading to scurvy. Vitamin C intake of less than 5 mg per day results in severe disease and death.

Sub-clinical deficiency occurs in otherwise healthy individuals when the intake of ascorbate is insufficient to raise levels to the point where white blood cells are saturated and vitamin C is excreted. This level approximates the RDA, although it would vary with the individual.

Base-level is when the intake of ascorbate is enough to produce blood levels such that vitamin C is constantly found in the urine. This level is necessary to avoid the hypoascorbemia [effects of the genetic defect preventing internal vitamin C synthesis] suggested by Irwine Stone.[37]

Dynamic flow is when an excess of ascorbate leads to incomplete absorption and excretion in the urine. This is necessary to avoid acute vitamin C deficiency in times of stress or disease.[38]

Pharmacological doses

Oral treatment requires ascorbate titrated to bowel tolerance, with large amounts of vitamin C taken by mouth.

---

[36] **Long, C. et al** "Ascorbic acid dynamics in the seriously ill and injured", *Journal of Surgical Research*, 109 (2): 2003, pp.144–148

[37] **Stone I** *The Healing Factor: Vitamin C Against Disease*, Putnam, New York, 1974

[38] Hickey S and H Roberts, *Ascorbate*, op. cit.

Intravenous treatment can be used to administer very high doses of sodium ascorbate for treatment of disease.[39]

[39] Hickey, S & H Roberts, *Ascorbate: The Science of Vitamin* C, op. cit. pp.130-131

CAUSING CONTROVERSY

"There is a principle which is a bar against all information, which is proof against all argument, and which cannot fail to keep man in everlasting ignorance. That principle is condemnation without investigation."
– William Paley (1743-1805)

Many in the medical establishment mock the public's love for vitamins and are quick to persecute their own ranks who use industrial amounts to cure patients. Paid pharma-lackeys in the media are only too ready to put the boot in whenever nutrition is concerned. Headlines such as *Vitamin C is powerless in the battle against colds*,[40] *Vitamin pills are useless*,[41] *Vitamin pill danger*[42] and *Are vitamin pills a waste of your time and money?*[43] reflect this creepy institutional bias. The approach is designed to cause maximum doubt in the citizen's mind that he can do anything himself to affect the outcome of an illness.

Credence has collected such statements over the years. Put together, they sound something like this. "Vitamins have been discredited as therapeutic agents. They are dangerous and might even cause kidney stones, cancer or piles. Those who believe in vitamins are deluded saps. Vitamins serve no useful purpose other than, ahem, stopping you getting sick, which is why they're called vitamins in the first place."

Say, what?

Yes, even those making such statements learnt in Mr Totton's history class what happened to sailors who didn't eat their fruits and veggies in bygone times. Yet the people saying these things are not stupid people. They *are* frightened people, nervous of losing power and all that cash. The threat to their incomes is real. A health revolution is underway as millions stop going to doctors on a regular basis and start looking after themselves better. As a

---

[40] *Daily Mail*, 18th July 2007
[41] Ibid, 6th July 2002
[42] Ibid, 30th August 2002
[43] Ibid, 9th July 2002

consequence, they are getting less sick and are living longer. In Britain, plans are being laid to raise the retirement age yet again. For some reason, the creepy people don't like this.

Let's talk about dangerous

In March 2000, at the Annual Conference of The American Heart Association, a report declared that high doses of vitamin C thickened and clogged the arteries.[44] This claim directly contradicted previously published, well researched reports, which stated that vitamin C in fact *strengthens* arteries, *reduces* thickness, and *prevents* plaque build-up in the blood vessels. The AHA declaration went on to receive the level of international media attention typical of such scaremongering, while the previous positive research, predictably, was given little oxygen. FR Kenner MD remarked decades ago:

"Some physicians would stand by and see their patients die rather than use ascorbic acid because in their finite minds it exists only as a vitamin. Vitamin C should be given to the patient while the doctors ponder the diagnosis."

Dr Klenner knew what he was talking about. He was curing viral illness in the 1940's using large amounts of the nutrient. He advocated a therapeutic use of vitamin C amounting to 350 mg of vitamin C per kilogram body weight per day (350 mg/kg/day), in divided doses.[45] A kilogram is about 2.2 pounds, so:

---

[44] **Dwyer J H, Nicholson L M, Shirecore A, Sun. P, Noel C, Merz B, Dwyer K M** "Vitamin C supplement intake and progression of carotid atherosclerosis", The Los Angeles Atherosclerosis Study, American Heart Association 40th Annual Conference on Cardiovascular Disease Epidemiology and Prevention, La Jolla, March 2-3, 2000

[45] **Klenner F R** "The significance of high daily intake of ascorbic acid in preventive medicine", pp.51-59, in: *A Physician's Handbook on Orthomolecular Medicine*, Third Edition, Roger Williams, PhD, ed. Keats, 1979

mg of Vit "C"	Bodyweight	Number of doses	Amount per dose
35,000 mg	220 lb	17-18	2,000 mg
18,000 mg	110 lb	18	1,000 mg
9,000 mg	55 lb	18	500 mg
4,500 mg	28 lb	9	500 mg
2,300 mg	14-15 lb	9	250 mg
1,200 mg	7-8 lb	9	130 - 135 mg

Which makes a mockery of the 60 mg RDA. Dr Robert Cathcart III, an orthopaedic surgeon and inventor of a widely used hip replacement prosthetic, advocated doses of vitamin C often in excess of 100,000 mg/day to reduce severe inflammation. In decades of practice, Dr Cathcart effectively administered such treatment to tens of thousands of patients, titrating the C to 'bowel tolerance', i.e. to the point where dosage brought on diarrhoea, indicating a saturation of tissues. Many of his patients used to suffer from arthritis, back pain, or injury; some had ankylosing spondylitis.[46]

Is all this safe? Andrew Saul PhD, editor-in-chief of the *Journal of Orthomolecular Medicine,* hosts two excellent sites on nutrition at www.doctoryourself.com and www.orthomolecular.org. In the bestselling documentary, *Food Matters,* he draws our attention to the fact that on average, not one death per year in the United States can be attributed to vitamins.

"Over a twenty-four-year period, vitamins have been connected with the deaths of a total of eleven people in the entire United States. Poison control statistics confirm that more Americans die each year from eating soap than from taking vitamins…. These statistics specifically include vitamin A, niacin (B-3), pyridoxine (B-6), other B-complex, C, D, E, 'other' vitamin(s), such as vitamin K, and multiple vitamins without iron. Minerals, which are chemically and nutritionally different from vitamins,

---

[46] www.doctoryourself.com/cathcart_thirdface.html & www.doctoryourself.com/titration.html

have an excellent safety record as well, but not quite as good as vitamins. On the average, one or two fatalities per year are typically attributed to iron poisoning from gross overdosing on supplemental iron. Deaths attributed to other supplemental minerals are very rare. Even iron, although not as safe as vitamins, accounts for fewer deaths than do laundry and dishwashing detergents."[47]

Compare that with death by traditional doctoring. The figures tabulated by Null et al below vastly exceed those owned up to in the *Journal of the American Medical Association* report mentioned earlier:

Condition	Deaths	Cost	Study
Adverse drug reactions	106,000	$12 bn	Lazarou, Suh
Medical error	98,000	$2 bn	IOM
Bedsores	115,000	$55 bn	Xakellis, Barczak
Infection	88,000	$5 bn	Weinstein, MMWR
Malnutrition	108,800	- - - - - -	Nurses Coalition
Outpatients	199,000	$77 bn	Starfield, Weingart
Unnecessary procedures	37,136	$122 bn	HCUP
Surgery-related	32,000	$9 bn	AHRQ
Annual Total	**783,936**	**$282 bn**	

---

[47] www.doctoryourself.com/vitsafety.html

You'd think the US government would be clamouring for a way to save that $282 billion, wouldn't you? No-one's interested. Why? Because sickness *is* the public sector – America depends on it. In Bill Clinton vernacular, "It's the economy, stupid."

Rats in the woodshed

"When one person makes an accusation, check to be sure he himself is not the guilty one. Sometimes it is those whose case is weak who make the most clamour." – **Piers Anthony**

Andrew Saul gives us ten ways to spot anti-vitamin bias in science and the media:

1. Has the journalist writing the article actually read the scientific paper? Are factoids being used or is real data discussed?

2. What exactly was studied, and how? Was it an *in vitro* (test-tube) study or an *in vivo* (animal) study? Was there a *clinical study* on people, or is its application to real life a matter of conjecture?

3. Follow the money. Who paid for the study? Cash from food processors, pharmaceutical giants, and other deep pockets decides what gets studied and how.

4. Check the dosages. Any vitamin C study using less than 2,000 mg a day is a waste of time. Any vitamin E study employing less than 400 IU is a waste of time. Any study using less than 1,000 mg niacin a day is a waste of time. All low-dose studies are set up to fail. Low doses of vitamins do not cure major diseases. Large doses cure diseases.

5. Check the form of supplement used. Was the vitamin used in the study natural or synthetic? Any carotene study using the synthetic form of beta-carotene only is a waste of time. Any vitamin E study using the synthetic DL-alpha form (instead of far more effective natural mixed tocopherols) is a waste of time.

30

6. Use the Pauling Principle: read the entire study and interpret the data for yourself. Do not rely on the summary and/or conclusions of the study authors.

7. Beware of Pauling-bashers. If a media article is critical about twice Nobel prize-winning Linus Pauling, you can be confident it has been spin-doctored.

8. Watch for these throw-away slams against supplements: "You get all the vitamins you need form your daily diet." "Vitamins are dangerous if you take too many of them." "Excess vitamins are just wasted by your body." "More research is needed before supplements can be recommended." "There is no scientific support for large vitamin doses."

9. Watch for pontifical public recommendations at the end of the article such as: "Vitamins can do some good things, but can do some bad things as well." "You are better off not popping vitamin pills." "Just eat a balanced diet." "If you take vitamins, take no more than the US RDA."

10. Consider *Saul's Law of the Media*: "Press and television coverage of a vitamin study is inversely proportionate to the study's clinical usefulness."

Load it in

High doses, even mega-doses of vitamin C are not toxic – period. Neither do they cause kidney stones or other such nonsense. *There exists not one peer-reviewed study anywhere in the medical literature which shows that any level of vitamin C causes kidney stones.* A scare like that, though, is very effective at putting people off. If you or someone you know has ever passed a kidney stone, you'll know boiling yourself to death in flaming paraffin while gulping down spoonfuls of cayenne pepper is carnal bliss compared to that torture. Robert Cathcart MD writes:

31

"Years ago when Linus Pauling wrote his book *Vitamin C and the Common Cold*, the critics immediately labelled the taking of large doses of vitamin C dangerous because it would produce calcium oxalate kidney stones. This practice of telling people that vitamin C caused kidney stones continues today by the critics of vitamin C despite the lack of clinical evidence of kidney stones in people taking vitamin C.

"It was hypothesized that since a significant percentage of ascorbate was metabolized into and excreted as oxalic acid that this oxalic acid should combine with calcium in the urine and deposit as calcium oxalate kidney stones. It is true that those of us who take large doses of ascorbate have elevated oxalic acid in our urine but no kidney stones. With the millions of people in the world taking vitamin C, if vitamin C caused kidney stones there would have been a massive epidemic of kidney stones noticed by this time. There has been none.

"I started using vitamin C in massive doses in patients in 1969. By the time I read that ascorbate should cause kidney stones, I had clinical evidence that it did not cause kidney stones, so I continued prescribing massive doses to patients. To this day (2006) I estimate that I have put 25,000 patients on massive doses of vitamin C and none have developed kidney stones. Two patients who had dropped their doses to 500 mg a day developed calcium oxalate kidney stones. I raised their doses back up to the more massive doses and added magnesium and B6 to their program and no more kidney stones. I think that the low doses had no effect and they, by coincidence, developed the kidney stones because they were not taking enough vitamin C."[48]

The half-life for vitamin C in the body is around four hours, which means that if you take 2 g at breakfast, by lunch you've only got 1 g left, 500 mg by tea-time and 250 mg by supper. Regular dosing throughout the day, therefore, is a good way of getting high levels of blood C built up. The level of vitamin C which can be maintained in the body depends on an individual's renal threshold for their blood, although some organs and tissues can safely absorb and store 100 times more ascorbate than the blood. Any ascorbate

[48] www.doctoryourself.com/kidney.html

above the renal threshold is either excreted in the urine as a result of the saturation, or oxidised and removed from the body.[49] Any levels above those usable by the body are quickly removed. Isn't nature wonderful?

[49] **Hediger, M A** "New view at C", *Nat. Med.* **8** (5): May, 2002, pp.445-6. www.nature.com/nm/journal/v8/n5/full/nm0502-445.html

DISEASES

"The diseases of the heart and the cardiovascular system are the number one killers of present-day Americans." **- Dr Irwin Stone**

If you are sick, one effective way of high-dosing C orally is to get a glass bottle (1–1.5 litres), put in 20-30 g of vitamin C powder (around 5-6 teaspoons) and fill with water, then drink throughout the day and replenish whenever necessary. This ensures high potency C is delivered on a regular basis simultaneously with water intake. Vitamin C is very safe for children and highly effective when they get fevers or childhood ailments. For adults, clinical evidence shows that mega-dose vitamin C (oral and IV) is effective for all forms of infection, flu, muscle weakness, muscle pain, chronic lower back pain, general pain management, periodontitis, and the more serious stuff we're going to examine in this section. Andrew Saul reports:

"Dr. Klenner recommended daily preventive doses of 10,000 to 15,000 mg/day. He advised parents to give their children their age in vitamin C grams (1 g = 1,000 mg). That would be 2,000 mg/day for a two year old, 9,000 mg/day for a nine year old, and for older children, a levelling-off at about 10,000 mg/day. As for me, I simply say, "Take enough C to be symptom free, whatever that amount may be." It worked for my family. I raised my children all the way into college and they never had a dose of any antibiotic. Not once. It is high time for medical professionals to welcome vitamin C megadoses and their power to cure the sick. Cure is by far the best word there is in medicine. It would seem that you cannot spell "cure" without "C." I do not think Dr. Klenner would dispute that."[50]

Because smoking lowers levels of ascorbic acid in the body, researchers theorised that vitamin C supplementation may affect blood lead levels in smokers. A clinical study was therefore performed on 75 adult men 20 to 30 years of age who smoked at least one pack of cigarettes per day, but had no clinical signs of ascorbic acid deficiency or lead toxicity. Subjects were randomly

---

[50] www.doctoryourself.com

assigned to daily supplementation with placebo, 200 mg of ascorbic acid, or 1,000 mg of ascorbic acid. After one week of supplementation, there was an 81% decrease in blood-lead levels in the group taking just 1,000 mg of ascorbic acid daily.[51]

Scurvy

Though images of toothless sailors and dentally challenged pirates spring to mind whenever scurvy is mentioned, Old Tooth Rot is still very much a modern disease, silent and widespread, and is rarely diagnosed as such because we're not allowed to call it scurvy anymore. Between 1497 and 1499, veteran Portuguese explorer Vasco da Gama lost over a hundred men to the disease on one voyage alone. According to naval records, between 1600 and 1800 over one million British sailors died of scurvy. Yet for hundreds of years the cure for this gum-rotting, organ-destroying disease was well known to peoples credited by the West with limited medical intelligence.

In the winter of 1534/5, French explorer Jacques Cartier found himself stranded when his ship became trapped in the ice in a tributary of the St Lawrence River in Canada. Soon his crew began dying of scurvy. Out of one hundred and ten men, twenty-five had already perished and many others were so sick they were not expected to recover.

Believing that the condition was caused either by bad vapours lurking in the hold of his ship or some malignant cause to do with the 'sea airs' (a common belief at the time), Cartier was astonished when help came from an unexpected direction. Some friendly local Indians showed Cartier how to boil pine needles and bark from the white pine, later found to be rich in Vitamin C.[52] His sailors swiftly recovered after drinking the beverage. Upon his return, Cartier

---

[51] **Dawson E B, Evans D R, Harris W A, Teter M C, McGanity W J** "The effect of ascorbic acid supplementation on the blood lead levels of smokers", *J Am Coll Nutr.* 1999 Apr;18(2):166-170

[52] Interestingly, the main ingredients in the pine needles and bark offered to Cartier's sailors by the Indians are contained in a number of beneficial antioxidant products available today

enthusiastically reported this miraculous cure to medical authorities but his observations were dismissed as "witchdoctors' curses of ignorant savages" and the authorities did nothing about the information they were given, except to log it into their records.

On a lengthy voyage to Brazil, Sir Richard Hawkins, the famous Elizabethan admiral, faced scurvy among his crew and discovered that eating oranges and lemons cured the condition quickly. However, despite reporting this phenomenon to the English authorities and to any physicians who would listen, the information was again ignored by the establishment. Sound familiar?

So deaths from scurvy became so numerous that by the 18th century more British sailors were dying from ascorbate deficiency than were being killed in combat. In 1740, British admiral George A Anson set sail to circumnavigate the globe in his flagship *Centurion*. Originally starting with six ships and almost 2,000 men, *Centurion* was the only ship to return. Anson reported that scurvy alone had killed over 1,000 of his men.

The great embarrassment this event caused in Admiralty circles prompted Scottish naval surgeon John Lind to seek a cure for the disease. On 20th May 1747, Lind began an experiment which dramatically demonstrated that fresh greens and plenty of fruits eaten by scurvy sufferers produced stunning recoveries. Later experiments showed that those who ate a diet fortified with these vegetable and fruit elements did not contract scurvy.

The reaction of the establishment was predictable. The Admiralty and numerous physicians, who were attempting to solve the same problem (and earn grants and fame into the bargain), barely acknowledged Lind's findings. It took 48 more years and thousands more scurvy deaths before Lind's advice finally became official Navy quartermaster policy. Ironically, after implementing this simple measure, the British, who became known as 'limeys' because of their new nutrition procedure, *soon gained strategic ascendancy on the world's seas*. After 1800, British sailors never contracted scurvy. The naval might of Britain's enemies, however, continued to be decimated by it, with the exception of the Dutch. Author G Edward Griffin surmises that the founding of the British

Empire in large measure *"was the direct result of overcoming scientific prejudice against vitamin therapy."* [53]

By the 1930's, purified vitamin C had been successfully isolated by Albert Szent-Gyorgi and scurvy officially consigned to the footnotes of history. For the correct cure to reach this status in Europe, all it had taken to conquer scurvy was 400 years of incompetence, millions of deaths, and finally the realisation that the answer did indeed lie in a simple diet of fruit and The Doctor Within.

Have we learned this valuable lesson? Of course not. The slower version of scurvy is now the leading cause of disease death in the industrialised nations, but you know it better today as...

Heart disease

Cardiovascular or heart disease is the umbrella term for any disease of the heart and circulatory system. This includes, but is not limited to, stroke, coronary heart disease, cardiomyopathy (the weakening of the heart muscle), myocardial infarction, arrhythmia, atherosclerosis, arteriosclerosis, thrombosis, angina pectoris, embolism, heart murmurs and hypertensive heart disease (caused by high blood pressure).

Over 3,000 Americans die *every day* from heart disease in its various forms. According to the British Heart Foundation it killed 198,000 people in the UK in 2007 alone.[54] Compare this with the number of road-accident-related deaths in the UK in 2008 (approx. 2,600), and you understand just how big a killer heart disease really is, not just in Britain and the US, but across Europe, Canada, Australia, New Zealand, China and Russia. There are predictions that all regions of the world will be affected by heart disease in a

---

[53] Griffin, G E, *World Without Cancer,* op. cit. p.54

[54] www.heartstats.org

similar way by 2020.[55] Currently in the USA it remains a bigger killer than cancer.[56]

As far back as the 1940's, doctors have been questioning the true nature of heart disease. J C Paterson, a Canadian pathologist, first suggested that the problem could actually be a result of vitamin C deficiency – a type of long-term, low-level, stealth-scurvy. Since then, other doctors researching in the area, such as Linus Pauling and C A Clemetson, have seconded this theory. Dr Matthias Rath, an understudy of Pauling's, writes:

"Animals don't get heart attacks because they produce vitamin C in their bodies, which protects their blood vessel walls. In humans, unable to produce vitamin C (a condition known as hypoascorbemia), dietary vitamin deficiency weakens these walls. Cardiovascular disease is an early form of scurvy. Clinical studies document that optimum daily intakes of vitamins and other essential nutrients halt and reverse coronary heart disease naturally. The single most important difference between the metabolism of human beings and most other living species is the dramatic difference in the body pool of vitamin C. The body reservoir of vitamin C in people is on average 10 to 100 times lower than the vitamin C levels in animals." [57] [emphasis ours]

Scurvy occurs when the collagen matrix in the body begins to break down. With heart disease, the scurvy process is much slower, sometimes taking years to develop. As Dr Rath reports, vitamin C is essential for the production of collagen and elastin, the elastic, fibrous materials which knit the walls of arteries and blood vessels together. Collagen fibres are a lot like the steel girders you see when builders are erecting a new skyscraper. Each fibre has been calculated to be far tougher and stronger than an iron wire of comparable width. Collagen cells form the structure for arteries, organs and skin, so a chronic vitamin C deficiency sees the commencement of a collapse in the arterial walls, necessitating a

---

[55] **Boon, N A, Colledge N R, Walker B R and Hunter J A** *Davidson's Principles & Practice of Medicine*, 20th ed., Churchill Livingstone, 2006

[56] "Chronic Disease Overview", www.cdc.gov/nccdphp/overview_text.htm.

[57] **Rath, M,** *Why Animals Don't Get Heart Attacks... op cit.* p.10

healing process in the form of lipoprotein(a) fats, which the body attempts to use to bond the thousands of tiny breaches in the arterial walls.

These lipoproteins are Nature's perfect Band-Aid. They are extremely sticky and form the atherosclerotic deposits associated with advanced forms of heart disease. Cardiovascular medicine, unaware or willingly ignorant of the underlying nutritional deficiency cause of atherosclerosis, focuses its attention on vilifying the lipoproteins' LDL (low-density lipoprotein) cholesterol content as one of the primary *causes* of heart diseases, when it is in fact the healing (survival response) precursor *brought on by a chronic vitamin C deficiency*. Today the drug industry has predictably mobilised a multi-billion-dollar business of anti-cholesterol drugs, which have wrought devastating results in cardiac patients, necessitating a further $20 billion drug program to combat all the side-effects.[58] Rath and Pauling discovered that:

> ➢ Vitamin C intakes (600 mg – 3 g daily), along with supportive intakes of vitamin E (800-1,000 IU), the amino acids lysine and proline, the B vitamins, essential fatty acids (EFA's), magnesium, minerals, trace minerals and amino acids, provide healthy arteries
>
> ➢ A long-term vitamin C deficiency will lead to atherosclerotic deposits in the arterial walls to cover the breaches caused by the disintegrating collagen, eventually resulting in coronary heart disease and, further north, strokes in the brain
>
> ➢ Vitamin C depletion over a few months will lead to massive blood loss through collagen disintegration, resulting in leaky artery walls, collapsing organs and death by scurvy[59]

Coronary arteries sustain the most stress since they are the primary roadways for blood being pumped by the heart. The need for ongoing repairs of the leaky artery walls produces an overcompensation of repair materials, such as cholesterol, triglycerides and low-density lipoproteins (LDL), produced in the

---

[58] **Sellman, S** *Hormone Heresy*, Get Well Int'l, Inc. 1998.
[59] Rath, Matthias, *Why Animals Don't Get Heart Attacks...* op. cit. p.23

liver, which lead to infarctions as this plaque builds up. Other areas, such as arteries in the legs, are also affected. Varicose veins often develop as a result of this ongoing healing process.

Autopsies of military personnel killed during the Korean and Vietnam wars showed that up to 75% of the victims had developed some form of atherosclerosis even at ages of 25 or younger. Yet those servicemen who had been captured by the enemy and incarcerated on rice and vegetable diets were later, upon release and a medical examination, found to have cleared the plaque during their captivity.

Victims of accidents are often found to have developed atherosclerotic deposits that would have become a problem had they lived longer. Dr Rath comments:

"The main cause of atherosclerotic deposits is the biological weakness of the artery walls caused by chronic vitamin deficiency [malnutrition]. The atherosclerotic deposits are the consequence of this chronic weakness; they develop as a compensatory stabilizing cast of Nature to strengthen these weakened blood vessel walls." [60]

For more information on the heart disease protocol, see the appropriate section of Credence's disease primer, *The ABC's of Disease*.

Cancer

Science knows a lot about cancer. It is the most studied disease of our century. We are aware that cancer is caused by environmental toxins, we know that cancer is a chronic disease, we know that all cancer patients have a parasite/fungus/yeast problem, and we know from Dr Otto Warburg, 1931 Nobel laureate, that cancer occurs when cells switch from oxygen respiration to fermentation. But there's another fact about cancer not so widely recognised by the public, and up until recently vehemently denied by doctors. Cancer is a metabolic disease. It is connected in some way to diet.

---

[60] Rath, Matthias, *Why Animals....* op. cit. p.57

Cancer is caused by a healing process that has not stopped on completion of its task. Cells damaged by mutagenic, environmental toxins divide abnormally, invading normal cells, proliferating without restriction, causing tumours that can be aggressive and invasive, able to infect and destroy bone. Tumours are essentially fungal material which has been duplicated inside fermenting cells. Cancer cells demand a lot of nutrients and can adversely affect the oxygen levels of the body. When cells do not receive enough oxygen, they revert to a primitive form of fermentation, releasing large amounts of free radicals as they metabolise sugars for energy.

In our view, vitamin C should be used in ALL cancer cases, both oral (titrating intake to bowel tolerance) and IV (intravenous). Studies show that when vitamin C is given intravenously in mega-doses, it is selectively toxic to cancer cells. Dosage varies from 30,000 mg to 200,000 mg IV/24 hours, sometimes more.[61] There are no reported side-effects aside from a dry mouth and a spacey feeling in the head. The treatment is thought to work by producing large amounts of hydrogen peroxide at the cancer site (massive oxygen). Recent press reports of the effectiveness of this simple treatment have rekindled the public's interest.[62] www.doctoryourself.com states:

"There are many good reasons to give large quantities of vitamin C to a cancer patient. Ascorbic acid strengthens the collagen 'glue' that holds healthy cells together and retards the spread of an existing tumor. The vitamin also strengthens the immune system and provides a surprising level of pain relief.

But there is more. Vitamin C has been shown to be preferentially toxic to cancer cells. Laboratory and clinical studies indicate that, in high enough doses, one can maintain blood plasma concentrations of ascorbic acid high enough to selectively kill tumor cells. If you have not heard about this, it is

---

[61] *Food Matters* documentary, www.credence.org;
see also www.vitamincfoundation.org/vitcancer.shtml;
http://orthomolecular.org/library/ivccancerpt.shtml
[62] www.dailymail.co.uk/health/article-362137/Vitamin-C-jab-combat-cancer .html;
see also Daily Mail, 5th August 2008 and 19th August 2008

probably because most of the best publicized (but worst designed) vitamin C and cancer studies simply have not utilized high enough doses. Now, however, Hugh Riordan MD and colleagues have treatment data which 'demonstrate the ability to sustain plasma levels of ascorbic acid in humans above levels which are toxic to tumor cells *in vitro* and suggests the feasibility of using AA as a cytotoxic chemotherapeutic agent.'"

For more information on cancer and the nutritional approach, see Credence's *Cancer: Why we're Still Dying to Know the Truth* and summary CD, *Cancer: The Latest Breakthroughs*.

Infectious Diseases

Influenza is not the only infectious disease that vitamin C can treat. Dr Frederick R Klenner was curing serious viral illness in the 1940's using high-dose vitamin C, both IV and oral. Today, his work is unknown by almost all doctors, so today, despite reasonable levels of hygiene, government media campaigns and a wealth of antibiotic-prescribing doctors, infectious disease plagues the modern world. One of the more serious examples is MRSA, a drug-resistant virus that all too often strikes in supposedly one of the most hygienic environments on Earth – the hospital.

The fact is, those with a robust immune system and clean and detoxified body do not suffer from infectious diseases. Chief causes of a depressed immune system will be lack of nutritious food, dehydration, vitamin D deficiency, food allergies, a constant intake of refined sugar and sugary drinks, and stress, which depletes vitamin C reserves in the body. Low levels of vitamin D are thought to be why we get most colds and flu in the winter. Optimising your diet and D3 (calcidiol) serum levels, plus ensuring good levels of C in the system, are the three best factors for avoiding these problems.[63]

Influenza is a common complaint, one that drives any number of people into surgery waiting rooms where they give it to everyone else. Often doctors prescribe nothing more than bed-rest, plenty of

---

[63] **Day, P** *The Essential Guide to Vitamin D,* Credence, 2010; see also **Day, P** *The ABC's of Disease,* Credence, 2010, "Common Cold and Flu"

water and lots of vitamin C. Yes, some doctors do prescribe vitamin C, not in any meaningful quantities or because they know specifically how it helps, but because common sense can penetrate even the darkened halls of Hades on occasion.

Dr Thomas Levy cites more than 1,200 studies in which vitamin C was used to treat infectious diseases successfully.[64] These included whooping cough, hepatitis, polio, common colds, influenza, ebola, herpes and pneumonia. Up until the 1950's, there was considerable interest in the pharmaceutical properties of vitamin C, but with the introduction of antibiotics, economics took over. Klenner postulated that vitamin C worked as a broad-spectrum antibiotic, activated the immune system and *"proceeds to take up the protein coats being manufactured by the virus nucleic acid, thus preventing the assembly of new virus units."*[65] If the cell dies and breaks down, vitamin C prevents these new particles from becoming virus cells. Vitamin C also strips away the protective protein armour of the virus cell, allowing the white blood cells to attack it.

Other conditions

So versatile is vitamin C that forward-thinking physicians should be engaging their patient's co-operation in tanking up for all occasions. The older you are, the better. Ascorbate therapy works by oxidising and removing free radicals, preventing the replication of viral cells, preventing oxidative cell stress, promoting the immune system by the production of antibodies and white blood cells, and strengthening the body against secondary infections that can kill. Consider what would happen if governments encouraged all hospitals and care homes to optimise their patients'/residents' vitamin D levels, ensured an 80% plant-based diet, 60% of it raw, hydrated them with clean spring water instead of Sunny Delight, and gave their charges therapeutic doses of vitamin C throughout the day. The world would witness miracles of Biblical proportions.

---

[64] **Levy T E** *Vitamin C, Infectious Diseases and Toxins*, Xlibris, Philadelphia, 2002

[65] **Klenner F** *Clinical Guide to the Use of Vitamin C* - www.seanet.com/~alexs/ascorbate/198x/smith-lh-clinical_guide_1988.htm

This is not rocket science. It's a matter of scientific and historical record that nutrition cures as well as prevents. Anyone who tells you differently is a menace. Why wait until ministers pull their heads out of their expenses forms to fix this? Each one of us has the capacity to understand what is at stake here and act accordingly. Britain could save the vast majority of the 200,000 deaths annually from heart disease alone with a little educated foresight. We invite you to do your own research, starting with the websites and resources recommended in the **Contacts!** section. The best doctor in the world is not the one charging £300 per hour, it's The Doctor Within.

FREQUENTLY ASKED QUESTIONS (FAQS)

Q: *What is the best way to ensure I have a vitamin C rich diet?*

Phillip: Ensure 80-90% of your diet is plant-based and organic, and consume 60-70% of it raw. Remember cooking food kills nutrients, especially enzymes and vitamin C. Eating raw may present problems for those peering out the window at three feet of snow, yet raw foods actually heat you better than cooked foods because of the preserved nutrient content. Steaming is OK if you don't steam the food to oblivion. Juicing vegetables is an excellent way of getting the family's raw food levels up with minimal commitment. Note that juicing is an art. You can juice so the results are revolting, or you can juice yourself to Nirvana. Everyone's heard of fruit smoothies; you can do the same thing with vegetables. What a tasty way to cram in all the fruit and vegetables needed for a vitamin C-rich diet – and one high in bioflavonoids too. Pick up a copy of *Food for Thought* or *Juice!* From the Credence store for more advice and recipe ideas.

Q: *I am healthy. How much vitamin C should I be taking?*

Nicholas: The long answer is, it varies from person to person, and also depends on your health, tolerance, stress levels, age and several other factors. The short answer is, follow Dr Saul's excellent advice of 1 g/day per your age up to 10 g per day. If you are moderately healthy but stressed, more will be necessary. Titrating your C intake to bowel tolerance will be a good indicator of how healthy you are. The higher the level, the more your body needs.

Q: *If I am sick, how much should I take?*

Phillip: It's down to the most effective way of saturating tissues, and that is unquestionably using IVC (intravenous C). Drs. Klenner, Cathcart and McCormick regulated C intake of their patients to bowel tolerance. In the case of cancer, this could amount to over 100 g/day of IVC. In the documentary *Food Matters*, Professor Ian Brighthope speaks of dosing patients on occasions up to a quarter of a kilo/24 hours (250 g). Seriously-ill patients should find a doctor who carries out IVC. This is available in most nations, though if politicians get their way under the UN's *Codex Alimentarius*, this might prove harder to find in the future.

The patient should consider oral dosage anyway. Nothing to lose and everything to gain. Follow my bottle suggestion at the beginning of the **Diseases** chapter. Also, in my book, *The ABC's of Disease*, I cover a wide range of illnesses and the most effective nutritional strategies to bring against them.

Q: *Surely if nature intended for us to take this level of ascorbate, she would have packed more C into her fruits and veggies?*

Nicholas: Nature probably did not intend for man to wreck his health using pizzas, slurpies, GMO, cooking, processing, irradiating and so on. In a perfect world (which we do not live in), an 'Eden' diet would suffice. In the stressed world of the 21st century, we have to get back to basics. The idea behind 'mega-dosing' C is to introduce a level of the nutrient commensurate with that produced by the mammal kingdom, adjusted for bodyweight. The great discovery is that vitamin C at these levels acts *therapeutically* (heals) with no side-effects. This is a huge bonus nature intended us to have. How do we know? Because it works.

Q: *I heard that vitamin C goes out of the system quickly. How can I stop this?*

Phillip: You don't want to. There are esterfied forms of C which have a slower uptake and therefore 'last longer', but basically C does what C does. C's half-life of approximately four hours in the body is an indication of how fast it works. In their book *Ascorbate*, Drs. Hickey and Roberts talk about regular dosing throughout the day to boost serum levels of C. For the 'techies' among you, if you plot the four-hour half-life decays of C on a spreadsheet when taking, say, 2 g every two hours, you'll notice the net serum levels increase steadily. This provides for and sustains the therapeutic effect.

Q: *What is the difference between the different types of C?*

Nicholas: Ascorbic acid, as its name suggests, is acid, and one component of the overall complex Szent-Gyorgi was studying. Too much ascorbic acid will burn the tum, so I favour a well rounded C complex supplement instead, which will include the ascorbates and bioflavonoids. And use powder not tablets. Tablets have binder and filler chemicals to bind the tablet together. Credence does an excellent powdered C supplement at www.credence.org.

Q: *When will the medical establishment wake up to this?*
Phillip: Next question.
Q: *No really.*
A: When enough of you are fed up with your loved ones dying unnecessarily and protest in your millions. I cover this subject in my book, *Health Wars*.

Q: *I heard that vitamin C contraindicates with chemotherapy in cancer treatment. Is this true?*
Nicholas: Yes. Chemotherapy consists of toxic drugs killing cells, both cancer and healthy cells. Vitamin C combats this action through the various modalities discussed in this booklet. Doctors know this and advise the patient, who has chosen the chemotherapy route, to give the treatment the best chance. Ironically, this means allowing the doctor to poison you in the hope of stopping cancer cell proliferation. It's not a great strategy. See Phillip's *Cancer: Why We're Still Dying to Know the Truth* for more details on this. Steve Ransom's *Great News on Cancer in the 21st Century* also covers this quandary in some depth. These titles are available through www.credence.org.

Q: *So the kidney-stone connection with high-dose C is a myth?*
Phillip: Yes. There is not one study on record that shows this. In fact, the opposite is demonstrated.

Q: *Vitamin C reversing heart disease is pretty spectacular. That's the leading cause of disease death! Why won't our legislators act?*
Phillip & Nicholas: Trust us, they are acting, but not in the way you would like. Legislators are the primary targets of the drug

47

lobby. Many are bribed to pass legislation favourable to their drug lords or offered lucrative jobs in Pharma-land following their government tenure.[66] Incensed by the huge loss of revenue resulting from the public waking up to 'self-help', the drug industry has actively spearheaded the *Codex Alimentarius* initiative via the United Nations to regain control over sickness.

Future legislation in your country has already been crafted severely to restrict your access to food supplements. Based on the lie that vitamins can harm you and must therefore be regulated 'for the common good' and prescribed only by doctors, any supplements available from health stores in the future will likely contain only meaningless RDA amounts. Codex is not being designed and enforced out of ignorance. These people know precisely what they are doing and the public is not protesting in sufficient numbers. The result? Unnecessary deaths will continue for the foreseeable future.

---

[66] **Day, P** *Health Wars,* Credence 2007; see also **Day, P** *Cancer: Why We're Still Dying to Know the Truth,* Credence 2009

CONCLUSION

Well, there you have it. A quick briefing on the C word. Naturally not a subject you can do full justice to in fifty pages, but do check out the websites in the next section and carry out your own research on this fascinating subject. Credence is constantly asked what, in our view, are the leading purges of 21st century humanity. Science spends millions doing studies on this every year but after 26 years of our own research, here are the problems:

1) cooked food
2) dehydration
3) lack of sunshine
4) lack of exercise
5) too much stress
6) too much toxicity
7) not enough knowledge

How much control do we have over the above? 100%! That's what the Credence mission is all about. We invite you to take the time to look at our other books, CDs, DVDs and briefing packs. They are loaded with useable, life-saving information and, like this booklet, have been designed to provide scientifically grounded answers to some of the greatest health problems we face. Also sign up for our free Internet EClub bulletins and weekly health tips (see last section on **The Campaign for Truth in Medicine**).

Today can be the start of the new you with a future full of knowledge and confidence. We are so lucky. Major answers have been found to some of the greatest problems dogging humanity, and we are confident that when the public gets to hear of them, they'll run with the information and pass the word onto others. Please help by being part of that process.

Good health!

Phillip Day & Nicholas Cockayne

CONTACTS! CONTACTS! CONTACTS!

If you wish to purchase more copies of this booklet or obtain any of Credence's other book, audio or video titles, please use the contact details below. Credence has local sales offices in a number of countries. Please see our website at **www.credence.org** for further details:

> **UK orders:** (01622) 832386
> **UK fax:** (01622) 833314
> **www.credence.org**
> **e-mail:** sales@credence.org

Obtaining health products
If you need more information or help with any of the materials discussed in this book, please use the above contact details.

Useful websites on vitamin C
The following sites deal with vitamin C dosage, history, ongoing political struggles and scientific studies:
www.orthomolecular.org,
www.doctoryourself.com
www.vitamincfoundation.org
www.mercola.com
www.naturalnews.com

Credence Publications
PO Box 3
TONBRIDGE
Kent TN12 9ZY, UK

THE CAMPAIGN FOR TRUTH IN MEDICINE

WHAT IS CTM?

The Campaign for Truth in Medicine is a worldwide organisation dedicated to educating the public on health issues and pressing for change in areas of science and medicine where entrenched scientific error, ignorance and vested interests are costing lives. Our ranks comprise doctors, scientists, researchers, biochemists, politicians, industry executives and

members of the public, all of whom have come to recognise that in key areas of disease, drug treatments and healthcare philosophy, the medical, chemical and political establishments are pursuing the wrong course with the maximum of precision, even when their own scientific research has warned of the dangers of these courses.

CTM STANDS FOR CHOICE IN HEALTHCARE

Millions today use nutritional supplements and alternative health strategies for themselves and their families, yet increasingly the public's freedom to choose is being eroded by government legislation and attempts by the pharmaceutical conglomerates to 'buy out' the alternative health market. CTM stands for the people's right to choose the healthcare system they feel is right for them, free of big business interference, pointless government regulation and coercion by the medical establishment, which often attempts to compel its own dubious remedies upon an unwilling public.

SIGN UP FOR REGULAR BULLETINS AND HEALTH TIPS!

Every month, CTM sends out EClub, its global online magazine, to keep subscribers informed of the latest news, developments, scandals and great news in healthcare and other relevant issues. Within EClub, doctors, researchers, journalists, scientists and leading healthcare advocates share their tips, views and strategies with hundreds of thousands around the world. EClub represents the news you are not being told; information that can literally change and save lives. Don't miss out on this vital resource, forwarded FREE to you every month! To join, visit **www.credence.org**.

HOW TO ORDER CREDENCE PRODUCTS

Credence has offices and distributors in many countries around the world. If you would like more information or wish to purchase any of the Credence titles described, please use the details in the **Contacts!** section of this book. Alternatively, why not visit Credence's comprehensive web-site at **www.credence.org**, which contains secure online global stores, a fully searchable database and many other great features.

Please note: Items not available in your regional shop may be obtained through our default 'Rest of World' store.

ABOUT THE AUTHORS

PHILLIP DAY heads up the publishing and research organisation Credence, which collates the work provided by researchers in many fields. He is the author of thirteen books on health and founder of the worldwide Campaign for Truth in Medicine (CTM). Phillip's speaking schedule is exhaustive and takes him to audiences all over the world. He is married to Samantha, has a daughter Anna, and lives in Kent, England.

NICHOLAS COCKAYNE began his higher education with a Bachelors in English at The University of Reading before taking a Masters in Creative and Critical Writing at Sussex University. His research work at Credence includes studying and evaluating political and technical claims published and presented to the public. Nicholas lives in Kent, England.